T0193913

FOR HE
HEALED
THEM ALL

Choosing Life - Choosing To Be Well Again

By George R. Williams, Sr.

WESTBOW
PRESS®
A DIVISION OF THOMAS NELSON
& ZONDERVAN

Scripture taken from the New King James Version. Copyright © 1979, 1980, 1982 by Thomas Nelson, Inc. Used by permission. All rights reserved.

Scripture taken from the King James Version of the Bible

WestBow Press books may be ordered through booksellers or by contacting:

WestBow Press
A Division of Thomas Nelson & Zondervan
1663 Liberty Drive
Bloomington, IN 47403
www.westbowpress.com
1 (866) 928-1240

Because of the dynamic nature of the Internet, any web addresses or links contained in this book may have changed since publication and may no longer be valid. The views expressed in this work are solely those of the author and do not necessarily reflect the views of the publisher, and the publisher hereby disclaims any responsibility for them.

Any people depicted in stock imagery provided by Thinkstock are models, and such images are being used for illustrative purposes only. Certain stock imagery © Thinkstock.

ISBN: 978-1-5127-8104-5 (sc)
ISBN: 978-1-5127-8105-2 (hc)
ISBN: 978-1-5127-8103-8 (e)

Library of Congress Control Number: 2017904558

Print information available on the last page.

WestBow Press rev. date: 04/18/2017

To the memory of my
beloved mother, Annie B. Williams,
who first taught me to say,
"Jesus wept."
But it was her consecrated and faithful
praying spirit that led me to
believe.

And to Gladys, the wife of my youth,
who, reaching beyond my faults,
still finds ways to minister to my being.

CONTENTS

CONTENTS

ACKNOWLEDGMENTS

First I thank God, who sustained and guided me through this work, and if there be any glory found therein, let it be attributed to and bestowed upon Him.

I now wish to acknowledge those who have encouraged and assisted me in this endeavor. I view this as a privileged moment to touch them. The totality of their actions and the time allotted in helping me realize this finished product has shown me a love well worth remembering.

I now make space for a special, posthumous tribute to three individuals who had nothing to do directly with the writing of this book but had much indirect influence upon it. They are Lillie Mae Walker, Savannah Strong, and Bertha Flowers Johnson. In a three-room country grade school (Brooks Avenue School, Shelby County, TN), they taught and schooled us far beyond expectations in an environment that was separate but far from equal. There were times when the heat from the wood-burning stove might not have been sufficient. And there were times when the water in the outdoor pump froze over, but we could always rely on your warm hearts to heat up and thaw these and many other chilly problems that confronted us, as well as your message: "Let's get it done anyway!"

You lacked educational materials for us. Some of us were from first or second generation families that were the first to ever attend grade school. Yet we were taught the basics—and taught them well. You overcame any lack of materials through the respect and discipline that you taught and demanded of us all.

Your service has
Served us well!
We are better men
and women as a
Result of it.
REST.

Stephanie and Deb,
Dad is thankful to both of you. You were there at what I like to call "the budding of my book," when my efforts may have shown little promise. I thank

you for all the early typing, guidance, and inputs that you gave your dad. Thank you, my Deb and Steph. I love you dearly.

George Jr.,
Ray, as we affectionately call you, I thank you for the time and effort you have taken to ensure my well-being remains well.

Each time Satan has made an attack upon my health, you and your wife, Marla, have been there to ward him off through your prayers and any other assistance I may have needed. You guys sheltered me for a month or more during my successful battle with cancer. All measures you have taken leave me exceedingly glad.

Thanks, guys. Dad loves you truly.

Thanks to my pastor, Reverend Sterling H. Brewer. Pastor Brewer, may God's blessings be ever upon you. You have been a positive guiding force along my journey. A good while back, I showed you some of my work that had appeared in an anthology of a local church. You read it and looked at me and said, "If you wrote this, then you can write a book! You should write a book one day."

Well, Pastor, I just want to say, "Here's the book!"

Posthumous thanks to Ms. Ida Heard. Ida, you were a beautiful spirit. For all your assistance in gathering and typing many pages in the middle and latter stages of this work, my written effort, my heart is filled with thanksgiving and glee!

Your untiring spirit and much-appreciated sharing of time are blessings that my heart will long remember! God bless you always!

Thanks to my sister in Christ, Joyce Dixon Williams. Joyce, you have worn many hats throughout my literary contribution. You have encouraged, advised, and imparted jewels of experience and wisdom to a brother making his entry into the narrative realm. Because you are a published author yourself, I have found it a great joy to work with you. As a Christian and the child of a pastor, double joy is mine for I know that you know firsthand all about the one who has healed them all. All my thanks, Joyce.

Last, I also want to give credit and thanks to Donna Phillips, Derwyn Golden, and all those individuals who encouraged me at the Maxis.

INTRODUCTION

This book deals with the subject of physical healing, which will be discussed from a spiritual point of view. It also takes a look at some of the crucial physical aspects of aging. On the other end of the spectrum, youth is also discussed. For youth and then age encompass what we call *life*, and is it not a wonderful, God-blessed life that we all seek?

The book also gives me an opportunity to offer personal testimonies of what faith and God's grace have done and continue to do in my life.

What does one do when faced with many of life's sudden and often disruptive forces? What does one do after being broadsided by a bad medical report or receiving a diagnosis that contains all the elements of a life-threatening disease? One can retreat to the dungeons of fear, denial, anger, and self-pity, or one can choose to live. What follows on these pages is a discussion of the latter: choosing to live and to be well again!

What I've written is not intended as the final word on healing, nor is it intended to set me apart as an expert on this subject. There is nothing here that you have not probably heard or read before. It is written in hope that it may strengthen you in knowing, as a fellow believer, what God's wonder-working powers can do in all aspects of our lives, especially in the areas of divine health and restorative healing.

I pray that the scriptures put forth here will awaken that seed of faith that has been planted in the spirits of all believers. I mean a faith activated not just to the point of believing, but one that is inspired to that marvelous point of receiving. Here I refer to that which was purchased for us by the death, burial, and resurrection of our Lord and Savior, Jesus Christ; through that purchase, we have been given the complete assurance of our salvation, prosperity, healing, and eternal life.

As for a brief testimony, I've been incredibly and wonderfully blessed to have lived more than seventy-five years without ever having been sick.

This does not mean that my body has not been attacked by Satan. During my lifetime, I have had four major surgeries. Three of these occurred after turning seventy. One of the more recent surgeries was a hip replacement from which I've fully recovered. I'm happy to report, thanks be to God, that on any given day I can be found walking briskly for two or three miles. This is not bragging—we believers call it *praise*!

The success of this discussion draws heavily upon the holy scriptures, for the scriptures contain God's word and will. It is His word upon which we must ultimately depend. Thus you will find a number of recommended healing scriptures at the end of this book for your consideration and study.

Because what we say and confess often goes a long way in determining what we seek and receive, I've included a suggested "Prayer of Faith" for your encouragement. Acknowledging God as the head of our lives, it is always proper and fitting that we call for His blessings upon all our endeavors and requests. Appropriately, the blessing from Numbers 6:24 is included in this work.

George R. Williams Sr.
Detroit, Michigan
February 2017

CHAPTER 1

Sometimes We Cry

Return and tell Hezekiah, the leader of My people, Thus says the Lord, the God of David your father: "Turn again, and tell Hezekiah the captain of my people, Thus saith the LORD, the God of David thy father, I have heard thy prayer, I have seen thy tears: behold, I will heal thee."

—2 Kings 20:5 KJV

O LORD my God, I cried unto thee, and thou hast healed me.

—Psalm 30:2 KJV

And straightway the father of the child cried out, and said with tears, Lord, I believe; help thou mine unbelief.

—Mark 9:24 KJV

The idea for this book came when I confronted a life-threatening disease. After having surgery, I was declared clinically cured by my doctor and his staff. This was without radiation or chemotherapy. I was—and still am—grateful for what he and all others concerned did for me. However, several days before the operation, by faith, I had received God's assurance that everything was going to be all right. Months after receiving my healing, I gave a testimony at my church that included a promise to print a list of scriptures that I used to pull me through this difficult period. It was also my prayer that my efforts might be useful in helping someone else along the way.

Upon second thought, however, I concluded that a mere list could, in no way, explain or justify what God had brought me through. Using God's holy word, I was led to describe the road I and many others traveled back to divine health after being devastated and ambushed by a bad medical report and subsequent surgery.

"I'm sorry," says the doctor, "but your test results came back positive. You have cancer. The full extent of the malignancy has not been determined, and further analysis will assist in exploring your options. In the meantime, here are a number of booklets on the subject that will help you understand the disease better."

After a few words of encouragement, he leaves the room, and you find yourself sitting there in complete silence. A few cubicles down, you overhear him telling a woman about her wonderful test results and commenting on the beauty of her little granddaughter. He says, "She looks just like you." At this point you feel that it is neck-wringing time! With every fiber of your being, you feel like screaming out, "Man, get back in here! I need you, and I need your help. This is no time to be talking about beautiful babies!"

At this moment you realize you are alone, all alone. After pulling yourself together and driving home, perhaps sometime far into the night, you will cry. Pity becomes your sole companion. *Why me?* becomes the great question that runs through your mind a thousand times, but it gives no answer.

At this time, what is commonly known as the "Why me?" syndrome sets in: *I have been a good person, and I've taken care of my family, gone to church, and paid my tithes. So I ask over and over, "Why me, Lord? Why me?"* This is the great "Why me?" question that has troubled men and women, great and small, through the ages.

Behavioral scientists and psychologists usually define this as the stage that precedes denial, which develops into anger, blame, and, finally, acceptance of the condition.

It is not my desire to get bogged down in a religious argument about why God permits certain events to occur in our lives. We know that God is sovereign in all His ways; if I or any other man could give definite reasons for all actions taken by God, then God would cease being God. Here I feel compelled to address a New Age rationalization in response to "Why me?"—"Why *not* you?" This line of thinking often concludes by asking whether or not you would want it to happen to your friend, your mother, your husband, or anyone else. *Why not you?* Such thinking takes the position that all human experiences are democratic in nature, thus bringing about a common sharing of these experiences that excludes no one. We are all one with nature or with a so-called higher power. Therefore, it becomes undemocratic (or even unfair) to disclaim any fate that might befall us, and sets us apart from our peers in terms of the consequences of that fate.

Sadly, I have known a number of people (Christians) who have been seduced by this line of thinking. They actually said, "Why not me?" when trying to find a reason for their illnesses.

The major consideration here is the fact that *courage* may and well should be exhibited in how we deal with an illness, but sickness, in and of itself, contains no virtue, valor, honor, or humility. A false sense of comfort may be found in the "Why not me?" question, but it is a comfort void of spiritual logic.

What if a gunman robbed you and, with full measure of his evil intent, shoved you down a nearby escalator? Would you jump up, in all your pain, and ask in response to this dastardly act, "Well, why not me?" I dare to think not! The reality here is that the robber and sickness operate out of the same bag; their objective is to steal, kill, and destroy. And it is Satan who controls this bag of evil. His eternal desire is to keep us confused, continuously making concessions over a victory that is already ours.

As born-again believers, we have a God-given right to question any disease or sickness that make its way into our lives—not only do we question them, we can pray for their removal. Exodus 23:25 (KJV) reads, "And I will take sickness away from the midst of thee."

Acceptance of Satan's plan of sickness is not where a blood-bought believer wants to begin his or her fight back to divine health. Such thinking should be rejected. In these perilous times of weakening and waning faith, our attention should be drawn to Acts 10:38, which tells us that Jesus—being anointed with the Holy Ghost and with power—went about doing good and healing all who were oppressed of the devil. Jesus is *not* in the business of putting sickness or disease on anyone. He came that we might have life and have it more abundantly now and forevermore.

Let's now look to the scriptures and see how God has dealt with this woeful "Why me?" matter. We read in 2 Kings that King Hezekiah was gravely ill and was told by the prophet Isaiah that he was going to die. The king, upon hearing the prophecy, turned his face to the wall and cried with flowing tears about his condition. And before he could finish telling God about all his good deeds and why he should not die, God stopped Isaiah from leaving the temple; God told Isaiah to return and tell Hezekiah, "I have heard thy prayer, I have seen thy tears: behold, I will heal thee," as written in 2 Kings 20:5 (KJV).

Don't be tricked into feeling guilty when attacked by Satan and his feelings of hopelessness and condemnation. Declare your redemption and move on in faith. Faith, sometimes in its most confused state, will produce victory when it comes from a contrite and pure heart.

We see a slightly similar situation of this faith principle in Mark 9:24, where a man brings his son to see Jesus; the son had a mute spirit that caused him to be thrown to the ground, often into fire and water. The man asked Jesus to have compassion on his son.

Jesus said to the man, "If you can believe, all things are possible to him who believes."

Immediately the man cried out with tears and said, "Lord, I believe, help my unbelief." Jesus then commanded the spirits to come out of the boy, and they came out, never to return.

Most assuredly, this event would have us know that the road called faith, upon which we travel, is always under construction and often in need of repair. It is God's grace, quite often, that allows us to reach our destination.

Jesus's most urgent task was not that of gathering followers but of keeping them out of the murky waters of doubt and unbelief once their commitment had been made. Even among the twelve disciples, this issue kept coming to the surface. Overcoming unbelief is one of the most difficult turns a believer has to make on the road back to sound health. As seen above, it is sometimes more difficult than maintaining one's faith. It presents itself more readily in the area of healing than any other aspect of our Christian walk. Ministers will confirm that sermons on financial or personal prosperity will generally create more glad faces of acceptance than anything they might say about healing. The prospects for a new car, a new house, or a husband or wife are all more readily believable because each new thing carries with it a reasonable possibility.

All the above things are provided for us under our New Testament covenant, which also includes our healing. But generally our approach to the car, house, or spouse reveals a wait-and-believe attitude: "If I don't get the new car this summer, well, then there is next year. I'll keep believing and working on it, and it will come. As a matter of fact, I know I'm going to get it! There is no doubt about it."

Could this not be called a great faith? We find no elements of unbelief in this pronouncement. The startling aspect of the above statement is that it is often made without the individual realizing that he or she is acting in faith. We often go through our entire life thinking there is something mystical about the faith principle—but there is not. Christ asks only that we believe when we ask.

There is another side to this issue, which we'll be discussing momentarily. Nothing is more immediate and personal than the status of our health. With good health there is the potential for every good outcome. Without it, all is diminished. For this reason our health becomes one of Satan's favorite points of attack—wellness is a condition over which we often feel that we have so little control. Our first defense against illness is unbelief or doubt, showing up in the form of "buts" and "I don't knows." This can cause one to think he is operating in faith when he is not. This thinking runs parallel to the above situation where the individual was acting in faith but not completely aware of it.

The conversation may go something like this: "The growth on the back of my neck keeps getting larger, and my uncle had the same kind of growth, and it killed him. I still have faith, but I don't know." In this case the seed of doubt has been firmly planted and will make it much more difficult for the man's faith to work on his behalf.

The other tool most frequently used by Satan to weaken our faith is suggestion. Suggestion, as he uses it, is designed to appeal to our greed and/ or pride, which we know as paths to destruction. He first successfully used this tactic of deception through suggestion on Adam and Eve, and the world has been wrestling with the sinful results ever since. We see this suggestive approach of deception in Chapter 4 of the Gospel of Matthew, where Satan tries several different times to tempt Jesus, who was finishing a forty-day fast and was hungry.

> *And when the tempter came to him,*
> *he said, If thou be the Son of God,*
> *command that these stones be made*

bread. But he answered and said, It is written, Man shall not live by bread alone, but by every word that proceedeth out of the mouth of God. Then the devil taketh him up into the holy city, and setteth him on a pinnacle of the temple, And saith unto him, If thou be the Son of God, cast thyself down: for it is written, He shall give his angels charge concerning thee: and in their hands they shall bear thee up, lest at any time thou dash thy foot against a stone. Jesus said unto him, It is written again, Thou shalt not tempt the Lord thy God. Again, the devil taketh him up into an exceeding high mountain, and sheweth him all the kingdoms of the world, and the glory of them; And saith unto him, All these things will I give thee, if thou wilt fall

down and worship me. Then saith Jesus
unto him, Get thee hence, Satan: for it
is written, Thou shalt worship the Lord
thy God, and him only shalt thou serve.
Then the devil leaveth him, and, behold,
angels came and ministered unto him.
(Matthew 4:3-11 KJV)

Our first and only defense against the wiles of the
devil is God's word. This is what Christ used. Can
we do better? You are lost. No, I'm found. You are
sick. No, I'm well. You are poor. No, Jesus died that
I might become rich. Stand on God's word and let
truth prevail. Satan is a hitchhiker, and in most
instances, he cannot harm us unless we stop and
let him ride.

Finally, much has been written about faith,
especially in these latter days. If assessed, what has

recently been written about faith would comprise hundreds or even thousands of volumes. There are books and recordings of all kinds on how to obtain faith, have more faith, use your faith, trigger your faith, sow seed to acquire more faith, and have that faith produce a desired result. On and on it goes, leaving many of us utterly confused rather than enlightened.

I'm inclined to rest my case upon the principles laid down by the author and finisher of our faith: Put your faith and trust in God. Fear not and only believe. And when you ask, do so without doubting, and it shall be given unto you.

CHAPTER 2

Taking God at His Word

God is not a man, that he should lie; neither the son of man, that he should repent: hath he said, and shall he not do it? or hath he spoken, and shall he not make it good?

–Numbers 23:19 KJV

And whatsoever ye shall ask in my name, that will I do, that the Father may be glorified in the Son. If ye shall ask any thing in my name, I will do it.

–John 14:13-14 KJV

For I am the LORD, I change not.....

–Malachi 3:6 KJV

Somewhere on this road to healing and a return to divine health, we must come to the full realization that God's word is true. Not only is it true—we must believe it's true under any condition or circumstance that may apply to us. In Malachi 3:6 (KJV), His word tells us, "For I am the LORD, I change not." There are any number of scriptures in the Old and New Testaments that adhere to this truth. If Jesus healed the sick and gave sight to the blind some two thousand years ago, He is certainly able and willing to heal today. He has never gone out of the healing business. Our role is reaching out by faith and claiming whatever we desire, whether it is salvation, deliverance, or healing. The work has already been done.

One of the meanings of the word *has* implies "that it is done"—an action has been completed, and the matter is settled. This is especially true when taken in the context of God's word and His will. Let us look at Isaiah 53, which proclaims the prophetic efficacy of Jesus's healing powers. In Isaiah 53:4, the prophet states, "Surely he hath borne our griefs, and carried our sorrows." The Gospel of Matthew gives us the fulfillment of Isaiah's fourth chapter.

When evening had come they brought to Him many who were demon-possessed. And He cast out the spirits with a word, and healed all who were sick, that it might be fulfilled which was spoken by Isaiah, the prophet, saying 'When the even was come, they brought unto him many that were possessed with devils: and he cast out the spirits with his word, and healed all that were sick: That it might be fulfilled which was spoken by Esaias the prophet, saying, Himself took

our infirmities, and bare our sicknesses.
(Matthew 8:16-7 KJV)

If He bore our sicknesses, then it means He took them, and we have no need to claim, carry, or tolerate them. Under this prophetic healing proclamation, cancer was (is) healed. Multiple sclerosis was (is) healed. Arthritis was (is) healed. Diabetes and high blood pressure were (are) healed. All forms of addiction were (are) healed. In 1 Peter 2:24 (KJV), the apostle Peter later agreed in this matter by declaring, "Who his own self bare our sins in his own body on the tree, that we, being dead to sins, should live unto righteousness: by whose stripes ye were healed."

Grasping and totally taking God at His word becomes the key to restorative health. God's word is the truth, and in the spiritual world, the truth will overcome any fact. The doctor's report says you have heart disease. This becomes a medical fact. The truth is that by Jesus's stripes, healing has been made available to you. To which of these two reports will you give more credence? Through the application of our faith and by the grace of God, discouraging medical facts can be turned into marvelous healing truths.

We must also consider that medical science, doctors, and hospitals are agents of healing in God's plan. The book of James tells us that all good gifts and things come down from above. Healing is a good gift! So we thank God for doctors, but our ultimate trust for healing, deliverance, prosperity, and salvation lies with God Almighty through what was accomplished by the birth, death, burial, and resurrection of our Lord and Savior, Jesus the Christ.

As a student at Michigan State University in 1957, I tore tissue in the lining of my intestines while trying out for the track team. The tear was not discovered until I returned home for the summer. My mother became very concerned after the doctor advised surgery. Her concerns were centered on the inherent risk connected with all surgeries, and she asked, "Might there be something else they can do?"

She also found it troubling that I was not scared. I had apprehensions about such an undertaking but not to the point of fear.

My first two years at the university were not easy. There were ongoing academic and financial struggles. Being a black man and coming from a public, segregated school system in Memphis, Tennessee, I encountered all kinds of problems competing with students from around the world—let alone competing with those from the wealthier cities of Bloomfield Hills, Grosse Pointe, and Midland, Michigan. I failed remedial writing twice. Required courses in science and accounting were extremely challenging.

On the financial side, my affairs were just as bleak. The little help my brothers were able to provide ran out before the completion of my first year. I cut my class load and found work as a janitor and roofer. Student loans, as they exist today, were unavailable. I was once asked what my quarterly tuition was, and my response was that I did not know because, whatever it was, I never had it when it came due. Thank God for the payment arrangements that could be made back then. No degrees were awarded unless all financial obligations to the university had been met.

I have explained the difficulties of my early college days to help my readers understand why I was not scared of surgery, and my mother had wondered at my attitude. I received Christ and the baptism of the Holy Spirit at the age of twelve at Riverside Missionary Baptist Church, Mitchell Road, Memphis, Tennessee, at noon, in the month of July. But in my early twenties, I had not developed a consistently prayerful life. Militarily speaking, I was still a recruit, not a tested soldier. Those early college years became my testing ground, where I had to learn to pray consistently in order to survive.

Thankfully, through it all, I kept a strong visualization of my mother in her long, flowing flannel gown, kneeling nightly beside her bed in prayer. This woman had many reasons to be persistent in prayer: widowed suddenly, overnight, at the age of thirty-six; left with seven children from age seventeen down to two and a half; and a blind mother-in-law. Nobody in our three-room shotgun house, which had no electricity or running water, had a job.

This visualization, even now as then, still helps to sustain me. From it I began to develop a prayer life that strengthens my faith and my faith walk. For it is indeed a walk of faith—a faith that allows me to know that Jesus loves me, and that I can fully take Him at His word in all things.

This trust has allowed me to look beyond being scared when confronted with four major surgeries and a long, worrisome list of life's other scary issues.

Claiming God's truths, let us move on to divine health and healing. We overcome the works of

Satan (and sickness is one of his works) by the blood of the Lamb and the word of our testimony, as written in Revelation 12:11 (KJV).

CHAPTER 3
On Aging

Oddly, we often retire only to find out that there is another full-time job awaiting us—trying to stay well. There are the insurance issues. What is covered and what is not? What about the copays and the supplemental insurance? Medicare— Parts A, B, and D—how am I affected by each? Once we work through these matters, real, time-consuming medical warfare begins. You know the routines—see the doctor, see the specialist; get the x-rays and the MRI. And don't forget the messy all-nighter, the colonoscopy.

Then there is the mental aspect of health. Only the mention of cancer can generate more anxiety than the thought of losing our minds to dementia or Alzheimer's. Most of us seniors have experienced the so-called senior moment, when we sometimes forget where we put the keys. We end up in a room and often wonder why we are there. Or we spend time looking for our glasses, only to discover we are wearing them. The senior moment! Is it something we should worry about? Probably not in most instances. Reason would have us know that we have been piling memories into our memory banks for decades; reason would also have us know that retrieval from an initial inventory can be accomplished more quickly than from a mature one, where memories sometimes may get misplaced or shelved in a remote corner, resulting in such questions as, "Where did I put my keys?"

Our short-term memory, where the locations of keys, glasses, and the thousand other things that we encounter in a day's time are stored, acts as a gateway and guardian over memories that are not necessary for our immediate or long-term survival. It makes sure that the main road (long-term memory) is kept clear so that we will not forget why and how we should run when someone yells, "Fire!"

So a little forgetfulness, here and there, is something all of us are likely to encounter as we mature. When a pattern of progressive forgetfulness and a consistent pattern of forgetting that one has forgotten develops, perhaps then professional help should be sought.

I've engaged this subject of memory because it is usually the avenue that leads us to the concept of being old. A person may reason, "I can't find my key, so I must be getting old."

Of course I reject the term *old* as it might apply to me. Yes, we grow older with each passing day, but we do not have to accept the common view of what it means to be old. The term usually carries with it the connotations of feebleness and decrepitude in both mind and body. It is my contention that God does not will such feebleness and decrepitude, and I make no claim to such either.

As I approach my eightieth birthday, there are certainly factors in all facets of my life that do not allow me to perform at the same level that I could at forty. I am grateful that God's grace has kept me and that if I reach one hundred or more, that grace will still be there and sustaining me. Stay prayerful and principled in all things, and God's goodness will take care of the rest.

Going forward, I think we all would do well to adhere to the comments of the late, great jazz pianist and songwriter, Eubie Blake, who lived to be one hundred. Someone once asked him to what he attributed his longevity. He answered, "I don't know, but if I had known that I would live as long as I have, I would have taken better care of myself." His admission is well worth remembering here.

Upon retirement, one of the biggest mistakes we seniors make is not maintaining our emphasis on remaining physically fit. I don't mean mowing the lawn, going shopping, and other such activities here. Yes, there is a limited benefit in such activity, but these activities do not address the most salient issues, such as pain in all parts of the body—knee, back, shoulder, wrist, and other locations. It is well known that as we age, there is a natural reduction in our bone and muscle tissue. This diminishment can affect such functions as flexibility, strength, balance, and coordination. Lack of meaningful physical activity can affect our immune system to the degree that we become prey to everything from the common cold to arthritis and cancer.

The above discussion was designed to encourage each of us to become engaged in a good exercise program that addresses and assists in warding off some of the ailments and conditions mentioned here. The good news is that we are never too old to get involved in such a program. Studies have shown that exercise and muscle conditioning improve bodily functions and good health at any age—yes, even at eighty! Of course, a physician or health care specialist should be consulted before engaging in any exercise program.

Please don't be too eager to join the electric wheelchair and scooter brigade. I believe such equipment is overused. Many of these chairs have been turned into personal transports with lights, bells, and whistles fully attached, turning up in all kinds of places. Just because the guy on TV says, "Medicare or your insurance will cover the cost," does not mean an individual needs one of these chairs. Rarely have I seen anyone on one of these chairs who appeared to be losing any weight, and usually quite the opposite happens. True, there are conditions where these electric wheelchairs and scooters are warranted and should be used accordingly, but people should not be urged to use them when such use produces more negative results—more weight gain and loss of mobility—than good effects.

This brings us to a subject that many seniors often fear—physical therapy. We fear seeing a physical therapist more than seeing a dentist. People may fear feeling too much pain for their old bones; who needs the pain for something that probably won't last very long? Also, doctors often recommend physical therapy as a last resort effort after the pills and other medications have failed.

Frequently physical therapy is viewed merely as a modality to try. This view obscures a certain truth. According to the American Physical Therapy Association, physical therapy is "a quality therapy for many conditions affecting older people, from Alzheimer's to urinary incontinence. In fact, one researcher did a study in which you had to be a hundred years of age to even participate."

As suggested above, physical therapy can restore or increase strength, range of motion, flexibility, coordination, and endurance—as well as reduce pain. I would strongly suggest a trial of physical therapy before investing in canes, walkers, and powered scooters. A few physical therapy sessions might well be a better investment. (By the way, Medicare and your supplemental insurance will probably cover most, if not all, of the cost.)

By the grace of God, I am a living witness to the benefits physical therapy can render. At seventy-four, I had hip replacement surgery to replace a worn-out hip joint. As noted in the introduction of this book, my healing was complete and fast. The surgery occurred in early May of 2010, and by September I was walking without a cane.

Almost everyone I knew (including some doctors) opined that it might only be a matter of time before my other hip would need surgery. (At this point I declared, by the will and grace of God, that this would not happen.) Some six to eight months later. my right hip started giving me trouble. Relying on my previous declaration, I went to see my primary care physician (not my orthopedic surgeon) and asked for a referral to a physical therapist.

The results of my visits to the therapist were quite remarkable. The pain and stiffness disappeared in a matter of weeks. My referral was for a six-week period. Since that time, I have remained in a twice-weekly, supervised exercise program. Two years ago, when x-rays were last taken of the hip, everything turned out to be satisfactory.

Aging comes ...
Through duration and the process for time,
Aging comes ...
Therefore, it is not what the process
of aging has in store for us
That matters, but what we do with it
When it comes ...

We should remain prayerful and proactive about maintaining our health during all stages of our lives. With this truth in mind, I would like to address my young readers on this subject.

Longevity begins at birth, perhaps even in the womb. All prenatal programs, which are designed for the protection of the mother and the unborn child, stress the importance of diet and other factors. The expectant mother is advised to eat well, exercise, watch her weight, and avoid certain unhealthy habits, such as smoking and consuming too much alcohol. All this advice is given to ensure, as far as possible, that the mother remains healthy and that the child will come forth healthy as well.

With a little deductive reasoning, it becomes very obvious that if a health-giving tactic works at the time of conception, it might well work at the ages of fifteen, thirty, or seventy. Mr. Blake's comments on his longevity holds very strong here.

Some of the best advice for the young on good health and longevity is found in Exodus 20:12 (NKJV) and Proverbs 3 and 4. The Exodus advice is as follows: "Honor your father and your mother that your days may be long upon the land."

As readers of the word, we often interpret *honor* incorrectly in this advisory context. It does not mean saying *yes, sir* or *no, ma'am* to one's parents, even though such responses are deemed respectful and proper. It does not mean helping one's parents up and down the steps. It does not mean cutting the lawn or even paying the rent. These acts are laudable, loving, obligatory responses that general human conduct requires.

Let's veer off the road into the high weeds for a moment to point our discussion: The reason some young people don't get old is that they die young.

Is that a conundrum tangled up in a paradox? Well, George Bernard Shaw, the great Irish playwright, attempted to shed light on the subject by saying, "It is a pity that youth is wasted on the young."

Our argument turns on the fact that premature deaths among the young, excluding hereditary and congenital defects, usually result from poor judgment, failure to heed sound advice, and attitudes of contempt and complete invincibility. The high teenage death rate from automobile accidents in this county is an example that must be considered here. Many of these deaths are associated with alcohol and drug usage. A large number of these deaths could have been prevented if proper counseling had been given and, more importantly, followed.

Gang activity, with its accompanying violence, is another example of this wasted youthful conduct.

Certainly, we cannot lay all the blame on our youth. They must first be properly instructed in the ways of life by a caring parent. "Instruct the child," the Bible tells us, for therein lies the essence of honor, which derives its power and influence from love!

To honor one's parent is to adhere to that parent's teaching and advice on matters pertaining to the conduct of life. A parent's word is to be accepted in the same manner as we accept God's word. We honor God when we receive and live according to His word. We express our love for God by the acceptance of His word.

Honor and obedience, along with knowledge and wisdom, are ageless and godly concepts that cover the sanctity of all human life. Everything concerning successful living is a concern of God, and He has made provisions to cover them all.

A portion of the book of Proverbs explores this matter quite well, concluding thusly.

Hear, my son, and receive my sayings,
And the years of your life will be many.
I have taught you in the way of wisdom;
I have led you in right paths.
When you walk, your steps
Will not be hindered,
And when you run, you will not stumble.
Take firm hold of instruction,
Do not let go;
Keep her, for she is your life.
(Proverbs 4:10–13, NKJV)

CHAPTER 4

Choosing to Live
For He Healed Them All

Now it came to pass in those days that He went out to the mountain to pray, and continued all night in prayer to God. And when it was day, He called His disciples to Himself, and from them He chose twelve whom He also named apostles.

—Luke 6:12-13

And He came down with them and stood on a level place with a great multitude of people from all Judea and Jerusalem, and from the seacoast of Tyre and Sidon who came to hear Him and be healed of their diseases. As well as those who were tormented with unclean spirits. And they were healed. And the whole multitude sought to touch Him, for power went out from Him and healed them all.

—Luke 6:17-19 NKJV

I call heaven and earth to record this day against you, that I have set before you life and death, blessing and cursing: therefore choose life, that both thou and thy seed may live: That thou mayest love the LORD thy God, and that thou mayest obey his voice, and that thou mayest cleave unto him: for he is thy life, and the length of thy days.

—Deuteronomy 30:19-20 KJV

Based on the above scriptures, our lives should be lived in a manner that embraces life long before we are confronted with the curse of a life-threatening or debilitating disease. However, because we live in a world where sin and disobedience abound, we often find ourselves not living under God's covering of divine health, which often leaves us exposed to the wiles and ravishments of the devil, resulting in all kinds of illnesses.

When this happens, we frequently find ourselves locked in a state of doubt, fear, and unbelief concerning the healing that has been made available to us by the death, burial, and resurrection of our Lord and Savior, Jesus Christ. But, thank God, through discipleship, prayer, and the exercise of our faith, divine healing becomes available to us all.

When we make Christ the Lord of our lives, we automatically choose life—for He is life. We are not talking about an abstraction or metaphor here. We are talking about L-I-F-E—breathing in and breathing out kind of life. We are talking about life as expressed in the crying of the newborn and the exuberant laughter of an old man. Christ is life. He is real—the essence of all creation. In John 11:25 (KJV), Jesus said to Martha, "I am the resurrection, and the life: he that believeth in me, though he were dead, yet shall he live." This text, properly interpreted, confirms Deuteronomy 30:19–20. The difference that exists is that between living under the law and living under grace. Christ said that he came to fulfill the law through the dispensation of grace and forgiveness. It is within this choice of receiving Christ that we live and move and have our being. Following the wisdom of this choice, we will treat our bodies as temples of God in which we strive to live a life of holiness. This choice does not lead us to abuse our bodies with drugs, alcohol, food, sex, or other addictive behaviors. Saint Paul admonishes us to let our moderation be known unto all men. This choice also teaches us about the benefits of proper rest and exercise for our bodies.

With all this goes an understanding that God is not a god who forces us to act. He is not going to make us do anything against our will. He does stand ever ready to help and deliver us in our time of need. He has promised to lead us and guide us—if only we ask.

Words of Healing

Therefore, when confronted by a doctor's bad medical report, be not afraid but only believe, for with God all things are possible. He has not given us a spirit of fear but of power and of love, and of a sound mind. Again, let not your heart be troubled, neither let it be afraid, for I am the Lord that healeth thee!

In further support of our faith, we read in Acts 10:38 (NKJV) how God anointed Jesus of

Nazareth with the Holy Ghost and with power, and Jesus "went about doing good, and healing all that were oppressed of the devil." Under this anointing, Jesus became the world's first and most prolific serial healer. Preaching the gospel of the kingdom, He went about healing all manner of sickness and disease. He arrested a stubborn and sickening fever and defeated paralysis. He cleansed lepers and gave sight to blind eyes. He restored speech to frozen tongues and hearing to deaf ears. He restored the function of withered hands and lame feet. A woman who had suffered a bleeding disorder for twelve years was made whole by the touch of His garment. A handicapped woman who had been bent double for eighteen years, at His touch, was able to stand straight. Devils, demons, and evil spirits were cast out; a raging lunatic, after encountering Jesus, was found "sitting and clothed, and in his right mind." Not only did Jesus heal; on three recorded occasions He raised the dead!

So the remedy for our sickness and infirmities has been revealed and documented in God's word. As the songwriter has noted, "Our healing has been preapproved. The work has already been done." Our task is believing and knowing that His word is true. And through it all, knowing that God is still God, that He loves us, and that as Jehovah Rapha, He is the Lord who heals us. Finally, the prophet Isaiah, some seven hundred or more years before the coming of Christ, summed it all up.

> *Surely he hath borne our griefs, and carried our sorrows: yet we did esteem him stricken, smitten of God, and afflicted. But he was wounded for our transgressions, he was bruised for our*

iniquities: the chastisement of our peace was upon him; and with his stripes we are healed. (Isaiah 53:4 KJV)

Now isn't that good news?

Amen.

Prayer of Faith
(confession)

I declare before heaven and earth and all the demons of hell that I believe I've received healing for this sickness, (name your sickness, whether it's heart disease, liver trouble, cancer, or stomach ulcers—whatever it is). I further confess that, according to Deuteronomy 28:61, this illness, (name it), falls under the curse of the law. But according to Galatians 3:13, Christ has redeemed me from the curse of the law. Therefore, I confess I am redeemed from this disease, (name it). I am redeemed. I am healed. Thank you, Father. Thank you, Lord! In the name of your Son, Jesus, I ask and receive.

Sign your name.

_____

This prayer should be repeated until your healing is manifested.

The Blessing

(Numbers 6:24–26 NKJV)

The LORD bless you, and keep you: The LORD make his face shine upon you, and be gracious unto you: The LORD lift up his countenance upon you, and give you peace. And may you walk in the confidence that with God nothing is impossible.

Amen.

CHAPTER FIVE
·•◆◆◆•·

Healing and Faith-building Scriptures

Old Testament

Know therefore that the LORD thy God, he is God, the faithful God, which keepeth covenant and mercy with them that love him and keep his commandments to a thousand generations. (Deuteronomy 7:9 KJV)

The LORD is my shepherd; I shall not want. He maketh me to lie down in green pastures: he leadeth me beside the still waters. He restoreth my soul: he leadeth me in the paths of righteousness for his name's sake. Yea, though I walk through the valley of the shadow of death, I will fear no evil: for thou art with me; thy rod and thy staff they comfort me. Thou preparest a table before me in the presence of mine enemies: thou anointest my head with oil; my cup runneth over. Surely goodness and mercy shall follow me all the days of my life: and I will dwell in the house of the LORD for ever. (Psalm 23:1-6 KJV)

God is our refuge and strength, a very present help in trouble. Therefore will not we fear, though the earth be removed, and though the mountains be carried into the midst of the sea; Though the waters thereof roar and be troubled, though the mountains shake with the swelling thereof. Selah. (Psalm 46:1-3 KJV)

Bless the LORD, O my soul: and all that is within me, bless his holy name. Bless the LORD, O my soul, and forget

GEORGE R. WILLIAMS, SR.

not all his benefits: Who forgiveth all thine iniquities; who healeth all thy diseases; Who redeemeth thy life from destruction; who crowneth thee with lovingkindness and tender mercies; Who satisfieth thy mouth with good things; so that thy youth is renewed like the eagle's. (Psalm 103:1-5 KJV)

My son, attend to my words; incline thine ear unto my sayings. Let them not depart from thine eyes; keep them in the midst of thine heart. For they are life unto those that find them, and health to all their flesh. (Proverbs 4:20-22 KJV)

The fear of the LORD is a fountain of life, to depart from the snares of death. (Proverbs 14:27 KJV)

A merry heart doeth good like a medicine: but a broken spirit drieth the bones. (Proverbs 17:22 KJV)

Death and life are in the power of the tongue: and they that love it shall eat the fruit thereof. (Proverbs 18:21 KJV)

But they that wait upon the LORD shall renew their strength; they shall mount up with wings as eagles; they shall run, and not be weary; and they shall walk, and not faint. (Isaiah 40:31 KJV)

Fear thou not; for I am with thee: be not dismayed; for I am thy God: I will strengthen thee; yea, I will help thee; yea, I will uphold thee with the right hand of my righteousness. (Isaiah 41:10 KJV)

For I know the thoughts that I think toward you, saith the LORD, thoughts of peace, and not of evil, to give you an expected end. Then shall ye call upon me, and ye shall go and pray unto me, and I will hearken unto you. And ye shall seek me, and find me, when ye shall search for me with all your heart. (Jeremiah 29:11-13 KJV)

Call unto me, and I will answer thee, and show thee great and mighty things, which thou knowest not. (Jeremiah 33:3 KJV)

New Testament

And Jesus went about all Galilee, teaching in their synagogues, and preaching the gospel of the kingdom, and healing all manner of sickness and all manner of disease among the people. And his fame went throughout all Syria: and they brought unto him all sick people that were taken with divers diseases and torments, and those which were possessed with devils, and those which were lunatick, and those that had the palsy; and he healed them. (Matthew 4:23-24 KJV)

Come unto me, all ye that labour and are heavy laden, and I will give you rest. Take my yoke upon you, and learn of me; for I am meek and lowly in heart: and ye shall find rest unto your souls. For my yoke is easy, and my burden is light. (Matthew 11:28-30 KJV)

And when they had passed over, they came into the land of Gennesaret, and drew to the shore. And when they were come out of the ship, straightway they knew him, And ran through that whole region round about, and began to carry about in beds those that were sick, where they heard he was. And whithersoever he entered, into villages, or cities, or country, they laid the sick in the streets, and besought him that they might touch if it were but the border of his garment: and as many as touched him were made whole. (Mark 6:53-56 KJV)

And Jesus answering saith unto them, Have faith in God. For verily I say unto you, That whosoever shall say unto this mountain, Be thou removed, and be thou cast into the sea; and shall not doubt in his heart, but shall believe that those things which he saith shall come to pass; he shall have whatsoever he saith. Therefore I say unto you, What things soever ye desire, when ye pray, believe that ye receive them, and ye shall have them. And when ye stand praying, forgive, if ye have ought against any: that your Father also which is in heaven may forgive you your trespasses. But if ye do not forgive, neither will your Father which is in heaven forgive your trespasses. (Mark 11:22-26 KJV)

And he came to Nazareth, where he had been brought up: and, as his custom was, he went into the synagogue on the sabbath day, and stood up for to read. And there was delivered unto him the book of the prophet Esaias. And when he had opened the book, he found the place where it was written, The Spirit of the Lord is upon me, because he hath anointed me to preach the gospel to the poor; he hath sent me to heal the brokenhearted, to preach deliverance to the captives, and recovering of sight to the blind, to set at liberty them that are bruised, To preach the acceptable year of the Lord. And he closed the book, and he gave it again to the minister, and sat down. And the eyes of all them that were in the synagogue were fastened on him.

And he began to say unto them, This day is this scripture fulfilled in your ears. (Luke 4:16-21 KJV)

Now as Jesus passed by, He saw a man who was blind from birth. And His disciples asked Him, say, Rabbi, who sinned, this man or his parents, that was born blind? Jesus answered, "Neither this man nor his parents sinned, but that the works of God should be revealed in him. I must work the works of Him who sent Me while it is day; the night is coming when no one can work. As long as I am in the world, I am the light of the world. When He had said these things, He spat on the ground and made clay with the saliva; and He anointed the eyes of the blind man with the clay.

And He said to him, "Go, wash in pool of Siloam" (which is translated, Sent). So he went and washed, and came back seeing. (John 9:1-7 KJV)

And it came to pass the day after, that he went into a city called Nain; and many of his disciples went with him, and much people. Now when he came nigh to the gate of the city, behold, there was a dead man carried out, the only son of his mother, and she was a widow: and much people of the city was with her. And when the Lord saw her, he had compassion on her, and said unto her, Weep not. And he came and touched the bier: and they that bare him stood still. And he said, Young man, I say unto thee, Arise. And he that was dead sat up, and began to speak. And he delivered him to his mother. And there came a fear on all: and they glorified God, saying, That a great prophet is risen up among us; and, That God hath visited his people. (Luke 7:11-16 KJV).

If ye abide in me, and my words abide in you, ye shall ask what ye will, and it shall be done unto you. (John 15:7 KJV)

Christ hath redeemed us from the curse of the law, being made a curse for us: for it is written, Cursed is every one that hangeth on a tree: That the blessing of Abraham might come on the Gentiles through Jesus Christ; that we might receive the promise of the Spirit through faith. (Galatians 3:13-14, 29 KJV)

And if ye be Christ's, then are ye Abraham's seed, and heirs according to the promise. (Galatians 3:29 KJV)

I can do all things through Christ who strengthens. (Philippians 4:13 NKJV)

Forasmuch then as the children are partakers of flesh and blood, he also himself likewise took part of the same; that through death he might destroy him that had the power of death, that is, the devil; And deliver them who through fear of death were all their lifetime subject to bondage. (Hebrews 2:14-15 KJV)

Seeing then that we have a great high priest, that is passed into the heavens, Jesus the Son of God, let us hold fast our profession. For we have not an high priest which cannot be touched with the feeling of our infirmities; but was in all points tempted like as we are, yet without sin. (Hebrews 4:14-15 KJV)

Cast not away therefore your confidence, which hath great recompence of reward. For ye have need of patience, that, after ye have done the will of God, ye might receive the promise. (Hebrews 10:35-36 KJV)

Now faith is the substance of things hoped for, the evidence of things not seen. (Hebrews 11:1 KJV)

Jesus Christ the same yesterday, and to day, and for ever. (Hebrews 13:8 KJV)

Is any sick among you? let him call for the elders of the church; and let them pray over him, anointing him with oil in the name of the Lord: And the prayer of faith shall save the sick, and the Lord shall raise him up; and if he have committed sins, they shall be forgiven him. Confess your faults one to another, and pray one for another, that ye may be healed. The effectual fervent prayer of a righteous man availeth much. (James 5:14-16 KJV)

These things have I written unto you that believe on the name of the Son of God; that ye may know that ye have eternal life, and that ye may believe on the name of the Son of God. And this is the confidence that we have in him, that, if we ask any thing according to his will, he heareth us: And if we know that he hear us, whatsoever we ask, we know that we have the petitions that we desired of him. (1 John 5:13-15 KJV)

ABOUT THE AUTHOR

George R. Williams Sr. was born and raised in the environs of Memphis, Tennessee, and received his early schooling in the education systems there.

At the age of twenty, he moved to Detroit, Michigan with his family, where he still resides as of today. He became a student at Michigan State University in 1956 and remained as such until being drafted into the U.S. Army in 1958. Upon returning home two years later, he re-entered Michigan State University, and went on to receive a Bachelor of Arts Degree in Political Science in 1963

In October 1965, George was wedded to Gladys Wilks of Gallatan, Tennessee, they were blessed with three children: George Jr., Deborah and Stephanie.

In the work force, George has served as an educator and corrections officer. He also has deep interest in the development of young entrepreneurs, and has spent a good part of the last twenty-five years advancing this effort. He presently serves as a mentor and advisor at three internet based service companies.

His literary interest first budded while in the military, when he was asked by some of his fellow soldiers to help with the writing of their "sweetheart" letters to their girlfriends back home.

During the early nineteen-sixties, as a student at Michigan State University, George participated in the writing of an on campus play titled "The Man Called Nigger", which was reviewed favorably in Ebony Magazine as part of a story it was doing about Ernest Green, who was a member of the group of black students that integrated Central High School in Little Rock, Arkansas in 1957. Mr. Green is a graduate of MSU.

George was a member of Pride Greeting Card Company of Detroit for a period during the nineteen-seventies. The company created, manufactured, and distributed a full line of Black greeting cards at the local and national level. He is presently compiling poems, aphorisms and posters written by him for future publication.

In 1956, George came under the pastoral ship of the late Reverend Roger W. Dixon, when he joined King David Missionary Baptist Church located in Detroit Michigan. The Pastor envisioned great things for George and shortly thereafter he became the first chairman of the churches trustee board. He still serves faithfully under the leadership of the Reverend Sterling H. Brewer

Printed in the United States
by Bookmasters

Printed in the United States
By Bookmasters